CW00403749

Holy Orders
The Image of Christ

by
Fr Jerome Bertram

All booklets are published thanks to the generous support of the members of the Catholic Truth Society

CATHOLIC TRUTH SOCIETY
PUBLISHERS TO THE HOLY SEE

CONTENTS

1. A new Priesthood, in the Life of Christ 3

2. Early Christian Clergy 9

3. The nature of Holy Order 17
   The Path to Priesthood 22
   Permanent Deacons 28
   The Rites of Ordination - Matter and Form 29

4. Life and Work of a Priest or a Deacon 35
   The Mass in the Life of the Priest 36
   Prayer and the Divine Office 39
   Sacraments and Sacramentals 40
   Preaching 42
   Pastoral Care 44
   Special Ministries 45
   Celibacy and Women 46
   Scandals in the Priesthood - towards a solution 50
   Prayer and Recreation 54

5. Further Reading 57

1. A NEW PRIESTHOOD, IN THE LIFE OF CHRIST

'**B**ut now Christ has come, as the high priest of all the blessings which were to come'. (*Heb* 9:11) His priesthood lasts for ever, and remains in His body, the Church. The Church, like a human body, is made up of many parts, each performing its proper function, and so we find that the priestly role of Christ is carried out by certain members of the Church, just as other members are teachers, healers, administrators, prophets and interpreters (cf. *1 Cor* chapter 12). The Sacrament of Holy Order, although consisting of a number of degrees, is centered and focused on the priesthood, so it is the priesthood that will occupy most of our attention.

chosen from God's people to represent them before God, and to represent God before them

We must begin by looking at the Bible, to see what priesthood meant under the Old Covenant, and how the revelation in Christ perfects and transforms the idea of priesthood.

The Old Testament tells us much about the office and function of priests: they are the ones chosen from God's people to represent them before God, and to represent God before them. They alone are entrusted with offering the sacrifice, and anyone who is not a priest is severely punished for attempting to do so (*Num* 16; *2 Chron* 26:16-20). The entire community of the faithful is a 'kingdom of priests, a consecrated people', (*Exod* 19:6, quoted in *1 Peter* 2:9) because the priestly function exists within it, and serves to sanctify it. The Old Testament ritual books (Exodus to Deuteronomy) describe many different ceremonies, with different names, all grouped together under the one English word 'sacrifice'. What they have in common is that through material objects, principally food, the holiness of God is mediated to His people, so by participating in the sacrifice they become holy. In the same way, pagan religions had priests and sacrifices, which were understood on the same principle, though involving false gods.

The Old Testament sacrifices and priesthood are seen in the New Testament as symbols or fore-shadowings of the one sacrifice of Christ, and His supreme high priesthood. The epistle to the Hebrews in particular contains a meditation on Old Testament texts about priesthood, contrasting the old and the new. The old sacrifices were not empowered to take away sins (only ritual faults): the

All the priests stand at their duties every day, offering over and over again the same sacrifices which are quite incapable of taking sins away. He on the other hand, has offered one single sacrifice for sins, and then taken his place for ever, *at the right hand of God,* (Heb 10:11-12)

new sacrifice of Christ does take away serious sins. The old priests had to offer expiation for their own ritual faults: Christ offers expiation for the sins of His people. The old priests came and went, all members of one family, whose genealogy is recorded: Christ is a priest like Melchizedek, not depending on any human descent, and who is a priest for ever. Hebrews is a difficult epistle to follow, being full of allusions and quotations from the Old Testament, and we need to distinguish the text from its commentary, but it does tell us much about how the first generations understood Our Lord.

It is not easy to disentangle just how the New Testament writers understood the relationship between the priesthood of Christ, and that of his apostles and their successors. This difficulty has led some to deny that there is any connection; they claim that Christ alone should be called a 'priest', and that all talk about men being priests is a later corruption of the Gospel. That is not, of course, the teaching of the Catholic Church. We do believe that Our Lord intended His priesthood to be exercised throughout all generations by a specific group of men, chosen and set apart for that service. In this way He fulfils His promise to be with us always, yes to the end of time (*Matt* 28:20), for it is the priesthood that gives us the Eucharist, in which we are made present at the saving moment of Christ's birth, death and resurrection.

Difficulties in interpreting the New Testament are partly due to the complexities of language and translation. The standard Greek word for 'priest', *hierevs,* was that used for the ritual priests of the Jerusalem Temple, men like Annas and Caiaphas, descended from Aaron, whereas none of the Apostles were priests in that definition. The preferred term in the New Testament is *presbyteros,* which is often translated 'elder', though St Paul does draw attention to its root meaning of 'ambassador' (*2 Cor* 5:20, *Eph* 6:20). Our English word 'priest' clearly derives from it. (The Latin equivalents of the two words are *sacerdos* and *presbyter* - as we shall see later, the distinction can be very important.) It is only in St John's Apocalypse that a clear link is made between a *presbyteros* and a *hierevs,* for the author recalls how he himself and his fellow 'elders' have been 'made priests to God' (*Apoc* 1:6), and a little later on the four and twenty elders (*presbyteroi*) are also 'made priests' (*Apoc* 5:10). St Paul also appropriates priestly language, using the cognate verb: 'the grace that has been given to me from God to make me a servant of the liturgy (*leitourgon*) of Christ Jesus towards the nations, doing a priestly work (*hierourgonta*) with the

New Testament words used to mean priest:
Hierevs: meaning ritual priest like those in the temple.
Presbyteros: meaning elder or ambassador.

good news of God, so that the sacrifice of the nations may be acceptable' (*Rom* 15:16). Certainly the Eucharist was understood as fulfilling the Old Testament sacrifices, replacing them, and perfecting what was only foreshadowed in the Old Law: 'we have a sacrificial altar, from which those who serve the tent have no power to eat, ...we offer the praiseworthy sacrifice everywhere to God' (*Heb* 13:10-15). St Paul also makes an explicit parallel between the Christian Eucharist and pagan sacrifices, when he talks about how those who eat the meat of pagan sacrifice enter into communion with false gods: 'you cannot participate at the table of the Lord and also at the table of demons' (*1 Cor* 10:22).

While priestly and sacrificial language in the New Testament is not always obvious, and has been interpreted in different ways, it is quite clear from the very beginning that there were certain men set aside to serve the Church in a way different from that of the majority. Our Lord chose twelve whom He called Apostles (*Luke* 6:13): they took care to replace the one who had fallen away (*Acts* 1:15-26), and then added others as the mission expanded (*Acts* 13:1-3). The second generation, including Paul, chose and ordained the third generation, including Timothy and Titus (*Acts* 16:3, 19:22). They in turn were to choose the fourth (*Tit* 1:5). All were selected and set apart by prayer, accompanied by the gesture of laying on of hands (*Acts* 13:3, *1 Tim*

4:14, 5:22). As well as this succession of 'apostles and elders', they chose and commissioned seven men to carry out practical administrative duties (*Acts* 6:1-6). These too were ordained with prayer and the laying on of hands.

Universal Christian tradition has seen the 'apostles and elders' as the predecessors of 'bishops and priests', and the Seven as the original 'deacons'. It has always been understood in the Church that the distinction between 'apostles and elders' or 'bishops and priests' developed subsequently to the New Testament period: St Jerome, writing in the fourth century, is explicit about this (*epistle* 146), and his opinion was generally accepted until the twentieth century. It is true that we find all three words, 'deacons, priests and bishops' (*diakonoi, presbyteroi, episkopoi*) in the New Testament, but they are never all found together. St Paul actually mentions a descending list of ranks, without using any of those three words: 'first apostles, then prophets, then teachers, then governors, then gifts of healing, then helpers, then guides, then types of speech' (*1 Cor* 12:28). Priesthood, or ministry within the Church, has been exercised in a different number of ranks at different times, but the Church has always affirmed that the unfolding of the Apostolic ministry into these different 'orders' is in accordance with the will of Christ living in the Church. (See for instance the Council of Trent, in Neuner and Dupuis, *The Catholic Faith,* para. 1708.)

2. EARLY CHRISTIAN CLERGY

In the writings of the second generation of Christians, such as St Ignatius of Antioch (d. 107) it is quite clear that there were three ranks of Christian ministry, namely deacons, priests and bishops. Collectively they are known as *kleroi,* 'clergy', from the Greek word for a lot or portion. This is not just a reference to choosing them by lot (*Acts* 1:26), but more significantly it refers back to Old Testament themes: the clergy are the Lord's portion; and the Lord is their portion (*Deut* 10:9, 18:1-2). They are chosen out of the body of the Church to serve God in a particular way, and should have no property or inheritance of their own, nothing to pass on to any posterity, for the Lord provides for them.

Detailed reflection on the nature of clerical order is not found before the great Fathers of fourth century,

> The levitical priests, that is to say the whole of the tribe of Levi, shall have no share or inheritance with Israel; they shall live on the foods offered to the Lord and on his dues. This tribe is to have no inheritance among their brothers; the Lord will be their inheritance.
>
> Levi therefore has no share or inheritance with his brothers. The Lord is his inheritance, as the Lord your God told him (Deut 18:1-3; 10:9)

though there are enough references in earlier writings to show that there was a real continuity from the earliest practice of the apostles to the well-documented and well-organised clergy of the great basilicas. Saint Jerome is a particularly fruitful source of information on the current understanding of Orders. As we have seen, he tells us that priests and bishops are essentially the same, but bishops have a fuller expansion of the office and responsibility of priests. Deacons, subdeacons and minor clerics are stages on the way to the priesthood, which grows step by step.

In the fourth century the lowest grade of cleric seems to have been reader or cantor, followed by subdeacon, deacon and finally priest. Over the next few centuries this graded hierarchy developed, until by the late sixth century a sevenfold sacrament of Holy Order was recognised. There were four 'minor orders'. Boys were admitted to training at the age of seven and ordained *porter,* given practical duties about the church from the very beginning. As soon as they could read, they were ordained *lector,* and took their place reading or singing at the Divine Office. The next stage was *exorcist:* little is said about this, but it was probably entrusted to the young on the grounds that they could be expected to be innocent. They seem to have been ordained *acolyte* at fourteen or thereabouts, given responsibility for serving at Mass. All of these boys were considered to be 'clergy', and had to live under obedience to those responsible for their education.

As acolytes they were expected to make the choice of marriage or celibacy. Those who chose marriage, usually at the ripe age of fifteen, would easily find employment as secretaries to lay dignitaries or merchants. They were still clerics, in fact 'clerks', and on occasion could still perform liturgical functions. It was presumably from their sons that the next generation was usually recruited.

On reaching advanced middle age (thirty five or so) they might feel that they had completed their families, and with the wife's consent (or at her initiative) could apply for ordination as *subdeacon*. The ones who chose celibacy could receive this order at twenty. After subdiaconate it was understood that the married must now separate from their wives, the unmarried could not now marry. Diaconate and priesthood followed at five-year intervals. Married subdeacons, deacons and priests, while required to live and sleep separately from their wives, were still expected to visit them and take their share in the education of the children, while the wives enjoyed status in the community as their husbands rose in the hierarchy.

The ruling that after the subdiaconate men must separate from their wives, and may not marry if they are unmarried, was for centuries universally accepted, and from at least the end of the fourth century was believed to be of Apostolic origin. (See S. Heid, *Celibacy in the*

Early Church, San Francisco, 2000.) Decrees of Popes and Councils constantly repeat the ruling, making it clear firstly that it was not always observed, but secondly that it was generally agreed that it ought to be observed. Clergy were encouraged to live in communities, where the young ones were trained, the middle aged could live in security, and the elderly were tended: rules for such communities survive from the eighth and ninth centuries, showing that clergy lived in many ways very like monks, though they were permitted to retain some private property. The essential work of the clergy was understood to be ritual and prayer: the celebration of Mass and the Divine Office, the administration of the sacraments to the people, and preaching. Other tasks, such as training the young, scholarship, administration, or the care of the poor, were important, but had to be fitted into time left over from the daily round of prayer.

> *The essential work of the clergy was understood to be ritual and prayer: the celebration of Mass and the Divine Office, the administration of the sacraments to the people, and preaching*

Change came in the Eastern church with the concession that major clerics could return to their wives as long as they abstained for a period before celebrating Mass:

thereafter clerics lived, as they still do, with their families, and community life in the East was reserved for monks.

The greatest change in the Western church came soon after the turn of the millennium, when the theology of marriage developed to the point that it was now seen as a sacrament, a holy thing in its own right, and it was therefore considered wrong to break up a marriage in order for the man to be ordained. The older practice became extremely rare (though never quite unknown), and the preference was to ordain only those who had never been married. Celibacy in this sense has never actually been compulsory in the Western Church, since those who have been widowed are frequently ordained, and in exceptional circumstances the older practice of separating from a wife can still be permitted even now.

In the first few centuries of the second millennium the great systematic thinkers we call the 'scholastics' developed the doctrine of Holy Order to its recognisable modern form. Order was seen as a single sacrament, received in seven stages, each with its distinctive 'matter' and 'form', culminating in the priesthood. Priest and bishop were still seen as essentially the same, and it was understood that the subdiaconate and all the minor orders were aspects of the diaconate that had emerged from it as needs arose. (E.g. see St Thomas, *Summa Theologica,* Supplement, q. 37, art. 2, ad. 11.) Each grade of Order confers a 'character' on the soul, so that it cannot be repeated, and cannot be annulled (although the exercise of that Order can be renounced or deprived). Minor clerics, married and working in the world, were reminded from time to time that they were still bound by certain obligations, and could still enjoy certain privileges, although it was no longer normal for them to return to the full-time ministry by separating from their wives and taking major Orders.

Although for various reasons the earlier ideal that all clergy should live in communities was eclipsed for a while, it was never lost, and from the mid-thirteenth-century onwards an increasing number of communities or 'colleges' of clergy were founded. Probably by the mid-sixteenth-century most diocesan or 'secular' clergy lived in these colleges, which had become much more popular than monasteries or friaries.

A big change came with the sixteenth-century turmoil. In response to widespread abuses and corruptions, particularly in England and Germany, the reforming Popes and Council fathers reaffirmed the doctrine of the sacrament of Orders, and clarified points that were in

Scholastic theologians analysed sacraments in terms of matter and form. The matter is the visible element or symbolic gesture, such as anointing with oil. The form is the actual words or prayer used, which brings out the significance of and makes explicit what is already there.

doubt. They also called for reforms in the training and life of clergy, introducing the *seminary* as the normal means of recruiting and training priests. This had the effect that all preliminary ranks of Order, up to and including the diaconate, were no longer exercised in public, in collegiate churches attended by large congregations, but were concealed within the seminary: as far as the general public were concerned the only visible order now was priesthood, and the rest appeared to be no more than markers during the course of training. Formal community life became less common, since the bishops now had much more power to move priests around. Parish priests still had the right to remain permanently in place, but they presided over a constantly changing group of curates, living according to the model of a great household with master and servants, rather than the older models of community and family. The sixteenth-century pattern survived reasonably well until the late twentieth century, when changing circumstances meant that most priests became isolated, living alone and subject to continual movement from parish to parish.

Great changes in the understanding of the priesthood and of the sacrament of Order came with the authoritarian Popes of the mid twentieth century. Pius XII, following a period of theological debate, ruled decisively that consecration to the episcopate was in fact a sacrament, and re-defined the 'matter' of the sacrament as the laying on of hands, in the case of deacons, priests and bishops, with the appropriate form of words. The handing over of the 'instruments' (Gospel book, chalice, pastoral staff etc.) is no longer considered to be necessary for the validity of the sacrament (Pius XII, *Sacramentum Ordinis,* 1947).

The second Vatican council ratified the work of Pius XII, and made a further change with the introduction of the permanent diaconate, now for the first time in the Western church conferred on married men without the obligation of separation. After the council, Pope Paul VI made even more significant changes in the 'form' of the sacrament, and in the Western rite suspended the subdiaconate and minor Orders, which can be understood to have been re-absorbed into the diaconate, and are no longer mentioned. In contrast to the former teaching of the Church, Orders are now generally understood to consist of only three ranks, deacon, priest and bishop, and priests are reminded at their ordination that they are in the second rank, subject in everything to the authority of the bishop. With the introduction of large numbers of married priests in England by John Paul II, another enormous change has come to pass, the consequences of which are still to be worked out.

3. THE NATURE OF HOLY ORDER

At the time of writing, despite clear teaching from the Holy Father, there is much confusion over the nature of priesthood, its value, and its exercise. The resolution of the crisis will depend on our understanding of the meaning of Ordination, and the status and function of the clergy. The Catechism of the Catholic Church sets out concisely what is now meant by Holy Order (Paras. 1,536-1,600). It reviews the Old and New Testament record, and sets the sacrament of Order entirely within the context of the priesthood of Christ, which belongs to His mystical body, the Church. A problem arises immediately in its use of the phrase 'the common priesthood of the faithful', which was suggested by the second Vatican Council, and has caused a lot of confusion, particularly in English-speaking countries. The crucial point is that there are two distinct words for 'priest' in Latin, *sacerdos* and *presbyter*. There is no easy way of distinguishing them in English, but the Council on the whole tries to keep them separate. Sacerdotal priesthood refers primarily to Christ: He is the only real *sacerdos* who mediates between God and humanity. In so far as the entire Church is the mystical body of Christ, the Church as a whole shares in His *sacerdotium,* which is therefore called 'common'. The *presbyterium* in contrast is a ministry exercised by only a few within the Body of Christ: it is 'different in essence and not merely in degree' from the common *sacerdotium*. Nevertheless it derives from the *Sacerdotium* of Christ, as indeed does every activity of the Church.

Unfortunately even the Council was at times inconsistent in keeping the two words separate, and the Catechism is even more so. The word *sacerdotium* is used in many cases to refer to the *presbyterium,* and the distinction which both Council and Catechism are trying to make remains obscure. This has led many commentators to assert that all baptised Christians are actually priests, that the restriction of specifically priestly functions to a few is a later development, which may or may not be desirable, and that in the absence of an ordained priest anyone may perform his functions. That is not what either Council or Catechism intended, but it is not easy to see why not.

Perhaps we can appeal to a metaphor, St Paul's favourite metaphor of the Church as a body. A human being may legitimately be described as a 'reasoning animal'. However in reality only the brain cells do the reasoning. If the brain is removed it is no use expecting the kneecap to take over the function of reason. Nevertheless, brain cells on their own would look foolish without the other innumerable types of body cell that provide support, nourishment and mobility. For the Church to be a priestly body means that certain individuals within it must perform priestly functions, which cannot be taken over by other members: yet, as Newman said, the Church would look foolish without the laity. (I hasten to stress that this is a *metaphor:* in describing the clergy as the 'brain cells' I am not forgetting the existence of some highly intelligent lay theologians and philosophers, such as

> *The exercise of priesthood is not dependent on the merits of the priest but, like any sacrament, on the faith of the Church*

Etienne Gilson or Jacques Maritain, and some very stupid clerics, such as.., well you know who.)

The Catechism, then, makes a distinction between the priestly nature of the entire Church, for all are members of one body, and the specific 'ministerial' priesthood of priests and bishops, which is not shared by the others, the 'laity'. 'The ministerial priesthood is at the service of the common priesthood' (*CCC* 1547), but it is not derived from the community (*CCC* 1545). The diaconate is not part of the priesthood, but is a degree of service, though it is conferred as part of a single sacrament with priesthood and episcopate (*CCC* 1554). Priests are essentially co-workers with the bishop, totally subject to him in all matters (*CCC* 1562-8). The Catechism goes on to reaffirm that ordination can only be performed by a bishop, and that it confers an indelible character. The exercise of priesthood is not dependent on the merits of the priest but, like any sacrament, on the faith of the Church.

Another twentieth-century innovation is the definition of ministry as three-fold, of sanctification, proclamation and administration, the bishop with his subordinate priests fulfilling the triple role of priest, prophet and king (or shepherd). As shepherd-kings they govern and direct the faithful; as prophets they preach the Gospel; as priests they 'unite the votive offerings of the faithful to the sacrifice of Christ their head, and in the sacrifice of the Mass they make present again and apply the unique sacrifice of the New Testament...' (*CCC* 1566, quoting *LG* 28). Previous generations saw sanctification as the one defining office of a priest, who is ordained essentially in order to celebrate Mass. In the past, preaching was seen as the responsibility of the bishop, who could delegate that responsibility even to those who were not priests or deacons (e.g. the early preaching Friars). Administration again was an episcopal responsibility, validly delegated to lay people. The function of celebrating Mass remains the principal and supreme work of bishop or priest: pastoral care and preaching may well precede the Mass in order of time, but the Mass takes precedence in order of importance. The bishop and priests represent the people before God, and God before the people.

In the mid-twentieth-century, certain writers tried to diminish that supereminent position of the Mass in a priest's life, and developments in the liturgy gave the impression that our understanding of the Mass as sacrifice had changed, with the result that many priests became seriously disorientated, and their spiritual life confused. Great numbers of priests abandoned their ministry, and an even higher proportion of lay people

> *The Eucharist is the principal and central raison d'être of the sacrament of priesthood*

ceased to attend Mass, since it was no longer seen as the essential constitutive sacrifice of the Church. There is no room here to explore the comparative theologies of the Mass, but we must note that the Church's teaching on the centrality of the Mass remains clear and unchanged. As Pope John Paul II writes, 'The Eucharist is the principal and central *raison d'être* of the sacrament of priesthood, which effectively came into being at the moment of the institution of the Eucharist... It is easy to understand how priests face the very real risk of losing their focus amid such a great number of different tasks... Priests will be able to counteract the daily tensions which lead to a lack of focus, and they will find in the Eucharistic Sacrifice - the true centre of their lives and ministry - the spiritual strength needed to deal with their different pastoral responsibilities.' (*Ecclesia de Eucharistia,* 2003, para. 31.)

This renewed emphasis on the central place of the Mass in the life of the priest and of the Church responds to a growing instinct of all Catholic people. That means that while acknowledging the undoubted truth that the entire Body of Christ shares in His *sacerdotal* work as Priest, Prophet, and King, these three functions are not intrinsically attached to the ministerial *presbyteral* priest, who is indeed always a sanctifying priest, but may only occasionally be prophet and king. Saint Padre Pio, for example, the best loved priest of the twentieth century, hardly ever preached, did very little administration, but devoted himself to the Mass and the Sacraments.

The Path to Priesthood

Holy Orders exist in the Church in two basic contexts, the 'regular' and the 'secular'. 'Regular' clergy are those who take vows to live under a rule, and are organised on a national or international basis within their own religious family. This means monks (like Benedictines), friars (like Dominicans), regular canons (like Norbertines), and Clerks Regular (like Theatines). The 'secular' clergy are those who live and work in this world, and are organised on a diocesan basis under bishops: for this reason they are really better called 'diocesan' clergy. (In between there is a puzzling penumbra of active priests who do not take vows but are to some degree organised on an international basis and free from the control of the local bishop: of these the most inexplicable are the Oratorians.)

Most parishes and missions are staffed by 'diocesan' clergy. These are normally recruited from young men who are specifically trained for the ministry in seminaries. In Great Britain, during the period when free secondary and University education was available, it became normal to recruit those who had already taken a degree. The legacy of this policy means that it may now take many years before graduates have paid off their debts and can start priestly training, during which time they may well have acquired undesirable characteristics which makes their training and deployment more difficult. In other countries, in contrast, it is normal to recruit young men as soon as they have finished secondary education, when they are much more amenable to character formation and training. This is one of the reasons why countries like Poland have such great numbers of priests that they can export them all over the world. There are countries, of course, where even secondary education is not available, so that anyone who wants to be a priest must be supported through years of basic schooling before his specialist priestly studies.

The Council of Trent recommended that the seminary should be an integral part of the bishop's residence, adjacent to the cathedral in the city centre. This meant that the students could become very familiar with the bishop, and could be seen constantly assisting at the Cathedral liturgy, and visiting the hospitals and schools of the city. While concentrating on their philosophy and theology, they would nevertheless still be in daily contact with the life of the busiest church in the diocese. This model sounds attractive, but has never been attempted in most English-speaking countries, where seminaries are isolated, and students formerly had no contact with the ordinary life of the Church throughout their training. More recently attempts have been made to integrate seminarians with parish life, and to associate them with secular universities. The results are still not quite satisfactory, which is why it is worth watching the new initiatives being explored in some countries. For instance in Paris and Vienna some students live and pray together in small communities, with a number of priests, very like the medieval 'colleges', while commuting to theological institutes for their academic studies. Modern communications mean that high level academic teaching can be conducted with no need for the students to be in the same place as the teacher, so that even rural dioceses could experiment: students could live in small communities, formed by a few good priests in prayer and virtue, and attend to studies on line if there is no major theological institute nearby, while having contact with the liturgy and pastoral work of a real parish.

That is effectively how regular clergy are trained. They join whichever congregation they choose, and live in a community house, with older and experienced members of their Order or Institute, absorbing their specific spiritual life, helping with the maintenance and running of the community house, and also learning the work of the community, while attending some specialist theological institute (either in person or by 'distance learning') for the academic side of their training. It seems to work rather better than the existing seminary system, and insights from the practice of religious orders might well be useful for the bishops in considering the future training of diocesan priests.

The process of selection of candidates is difficult, for out of many applicants, only a few can be found suitable. Certain basic requirements are obvious: the candidate should be in good health, both mental and physical, and of good reputation. The church should certainly care for priests who become incapacitated or infirm, or who have fallen into serious difficulties, but candidates should not start out like that. The candidate must be free from debt or obligations, either financial or family. He should also be capable of the academic study necessary for the priesthood. All these things can usually be ascertained quickly and easily, as the candidate offers letters of recommendation from those who know him well.

In many dioceses the actual selection has been made in a series of interviews and conferences, modelled on business methods. These have proved problematical, with good candidates being turned away, and some very strange fish allowed in, as we have seen to our cost. The problem, of course, is that business and management criteria are totally different from those of the Spirit, and the ideal candidate for a management post would be totally unacceptable as a priest. Religious orders have the more pragmatic policy of simply inviting the candidate to live with them for a year: it quickly becomes clear whether this is someone who is going to fit in and be suitable for that particular institute. Of course mistakes can be made, but the community model again looks more promising, which is why many dioceses now ask candidates to spend a preliminary year living in a community (a former seminary is proposed for this) before starting academic studies.

So Jacob served seven years for Rachel, and they seemed but a few days, because of the greatness of his love

Classically the training period for the priesthood was seven years ('So Jacob served seven years for Rachel, and they seemed but a few days, because of the greatness of his love.' *Gen* 29:20) This can be reduced, depending on age, and the nature of studies already completed. Academic training concentrates on theoretical philosophy and theology, to understand the teaching of the Church, biblical studies, in order to preach, and moral theology, to guide souls in perplexity.

Catholic theology is a very different thing from what is called 'Theology' in modern British universities, which may be more like comparative anthropology, not an adequate preparation for the priesthood. Practical aspects of the training should include proper celebration of the liturgy, pastoral care and understanding, public speaking, and catechesis; it also ought to involve book-keeping, cooking, driving and cycle maintenance. Languages are extremely useful for any priest: Latin, Greek and Hebrew are necessary to understand the extraordinary riches of the Church's tradition; while for ministry in a modern parish a variety of modern languages are all but essential.

Since the suspension of all Orders below the diaconate, the students in a seminary are simply laymen, with no rights. They receive the lay ministries of 'lector' and 'acolyte' on the way, but do not actually become clerics until they are ordained deacon, at which point they usually leave the seminary to start parish work. In contrast, members of religious orders are usually 'professed' in simple vows before they start their academic studies, and are therefore already members of their religious family. For a diocesan student, ordination to the diaconate is the irrevocable moment of decision: for a regular it is solemn profession, after which the diaconate seems less important. For both, the goal is priesthood.

Permanent Deacons

Those who want to be permanent deacons usually follow a very different course, though it may take place in the same seminaries at weekends. They (and their wives) attend a number of sessions, spread over three years, in between which they are expected to read and to write assignments. They are usually expected to be in full-time employment (the church undertakes no responsibility for supporting them), and so their training is very much part-time. The permanent deacon, therefore, cannot be expected to study in the depth and range required of one to be ordained 'transitional' deacon, hoping to proceed to the priesthood. The transitional deacon usually spends a year in a parish, learning the practicalities of pastoral work, and is confronted for the first time with the extraordinary people who make up a typical parish. It is not surprising that a number of those whose training had hitherto been rather isolated stop at this point, and never proceed to priesthood, or delay it several years. Normally, however, he is ordained priest after one year as deacon. Ordination is a ceremony of great significance, not only for the candidate, but for his family, his native parish, and the parish of his diaconate. It can be difficult to choose where to be ordained, with two or more parishes vying for the honour.

In a religious order, ordination nearly always takes place in a community house of that order, an abbey, friary or whatever. It is seen as a family occasion for members of the order, as well as for the candidate's natural family and the lay people served by the community, whether as parishioners or spiritual children. In a religious order, although the priesthood is fully valued, it may make little difference in the day to day life of the new priest: he has already for several years been a member of his community, and continues with the familiar routine of community life. For a diocesan priest, however, the transition from student life in the seminary to the raw isolation of the parish can be very difficult indeed, even if it has been tempered by a year as a deacon..

The Rites of Ordination - Matter and Form

The essential feature of ordination is still, as it was in the Acts of the Apostles, prayer and the laying on of hands. Additional ceremonies, some of great antiquity, have accumulated around these key elements, but if necessary can be omitted (e.g. in extreme danger during persecution) without making the ordination invalid. The ceremonies, including many picturesque features, were drastically reduced in 1968, though the old rites are occasionally used as legitimate alternatives when appropriate. For many centuries the custom was to use the word 'ordination' for priests and deacons (and the minor orders) and to speak of the 'consecration' of a bishop, to emphasise the understanding that episcopate was not really part of the sacrament of order: now the word 'ordination' is used of all three, and for that matter the word 'consecration' appears in all three rites. In the first millennium the words seem to have been used interchangeably.

For a **Deacon,** the ceremony begins after the gospel of the ordination Mass, when the candidate is called out of the congregation and presented to the bishop. A sponsor (usually the seminary rector) affirms that he has been found worthy to be ordained. (On a famous occasion the late Cardinal Hume then remarked, 'Monsignor has just told me a lie', and went on to explain that no one can possibly be found worthy of being a deacon, priest or bishop, on his own merits: like every sacrament, ordination depends entirely on the grace of God who alone can call and choose those He wants.) The candidate is asked to affirm his public commitment to celibacy (unless he is already married), and his willingness to be ordained as deacon, to carry out the duties of the office, and to shape his life accordingly. He then makes a promise of obedience to his own bishop or religious superior (who may not be the one actually doing the ordination).

There follows the great prayer of all the saints: the candidate lies prostrate on the floor, while all others kneel (or stand, in Eastertide), and invoke the prayers of all the saints in a litany of intercession. Immediately afterwards the candidate kneels before the bishop, who lays hands on him in silence, and then recites the prayer of consecration, in which the key words are:

> Lord, send forth upon him the Holy Spirit, that he may be strengthened by the gift of your sevenfold grace to carry out faithfully the work of the ministry.

The deacon is vested in his stole, worn over the right shoulder, and his dalmatic, and is presented with the book of the Gospels, with the words, 'believe what you read, teach what you believe, and practice what you teach'. After a sign of peace, the Mass proceeds as normal.

For a **Priest,** the ceremony begins in exactly the same way as for a deacon, with the calling out, testimonial, address, examination and promise of obedience, and the prayer of intercession of all the saints. Again, the bishop lays hands on the candidate's head in silence, after which all priests present come up one by one and lay on hands, still in silence. The bishop then recites the prayer of consecration, in which the key words are:

> Almighty Father, grant to this servant of yours the dignity of the priesthood. Renew within him the Spirit of holiness. As a co-worker with the order of bishops may he be faithful to the ministry that he receives from you, Lord God, and be to others a model of right conduct.

According to ancient custom, all the priests present hold their right hands towards the new priest, as token of their co-operation with the bishop in the work of ordination. The new priest has his stole rearranged in priestly fashion, and is vested with the chasuble. The bishop then anoints his hands with the consecrating oil of chrism, saying, 'The Father anointed our Lord Jesus Christ through the power of the Holy Spirit. May Jesus preserve you to sanctify the Christian people and to offer sacrifice to God.' Then he places into his hands the chalice and paten with the words, 'Accept from the holy people of God the gifts to be offered to him. Know what you are doing, and imitate the mystery you celebrate: model your life on the mystery of the Lord's cross.' Again there is a sign of peace, and the Mass proceeds, with the new priest concelebrating.

To ordain or consecrate a **Bishop,** whenever possible at least three bishops are gathered to ensure the apostolic succession. When the candidate is presented, his mandate from the Holy See must be read out. He is examined at greater length than deacon or priest, on his commitment to the unity and doctrine of the Church and his pastoral responsibility. After the usual litany, the principal consecrator lays hands on the new bishop's head in silence, and all other bishops present do the same, one by one. An open book of the Gospel is then laid on the head of the new bishop, held there by two deacons, while the principal consecrator recites the prayer of consecration, the other bishops joining in for the key words:

So now pour out upon this chosen one that power which is from you, the governing Spirit whom you gave to your beloved Son, Jesus Christ, the Spirit given by him to the holy apostles, who founded the Church in every place to be your temple for the unceasing glory and praise of your name.

The new bishop is then anointed on the head, with the words, 'God has brought you to share the high priesthood of Christ, May he pour out on you the oil of mystical anointing and enrich you with spiritual blessings.' He is then given the Gospel book, ring, mitre and pastoral staff.

4. Life and Work of a Priest or a Deacon

It would be presumptuous of me to say anything here about the work of a bishop, so I shall confine myself to the more familiar ground of lesser clerical life. Conditions vary, and the way in which individual priests or deacons live differs greatly, but there are some things we all have in common. First and centrally comes the Mass. Traditionally all the Holy Orders were defined in relationship to the Mass. The priest is essentially one who celebrates Mass, who offers the sacrifice, consecrates the Body and Blood of Christ, and distributes Communion to the faithful. The deacon is one who proclaims the Gospel: the other ministries each found their proper place within the sacrifice.

The **deacon** is a minister of service, expressed in his assistance at Mass and other functions, but also in his own right in the work of administration and charity for which the deacons were first appointed (Acts 6:1-6). A

It would not be right for us to neglect the word of God so as to give out food; you, brothers, must select from among yourselves seven men of good reputation, filled with the Spirit and with wisdom; we will hand over this duty to them... They presented these to the apostles, who prayed and laid their hands on them. (Acts 6:2-3, 6) permanent deacon is usually a married man, of mature age, well known in the local community, with a secular career behind him. Unlike a priest, he cannot be moved around by the bishop. The degree to which he is active varies very much from parish to parish and diocese to diocese. In many cases he has only a liturgical function, preaching, reading the Gospel at Mass, administering baptism and conducting marriages and funerals. Like many lay Christians he can also be involved in catechesis, charitable work, and organising the parish finances. In certain cases he may be responsible for the running of a parish or mission where there is no priest, particularly in countries under persecution where a married man with a secular career attracts less suspicion.

The Mass in the Life of the Priest

More than anyone else, the priest derives his spirituality and his sanctification from the Mass. Everything else he does is secondary to that one great duty and privilege, and nothing can take precedence over the celebration of Mass. It is in the Mass that the presbyteral priest carries out the essential role of sanctification, the very essence of sacerdotal priesthood. Christ gives Himself to His people under the form of bread and wine: it is the human priest who offers the lives and loves of the people along with the gifts of bread and wine; the priest who invokes the Holy Spirit to make that miracle present; the priest who descends among the people to feed them with the Body and Blood of Christ so that the entire people become 'one body, one spirit in Christ'. That is why during the Mass the priest acts in the person of Christ: the vestments veil his human frailty, and he 'puts on Christ' so that he can speak in Christ's name, 'this is my body'. Christ is present as the people gather and listen to the Scriptures, present too in the person of the priest who represents Him, but only in the Blessed Sacrament is He locally and tangibly present in material form. It is the priest, and only the priest, who can act as the human intermediary to make Christ present, for it is this action of the Mass that really defines what a priest is. All else that he does is secondary, all his other activity derives its meaning only from the Mass, as was so recently reaffirmed by Pope John Paul II in his encyclical *Ecclesia de Eucharistia,* already quoted.

Celebrating Mass can be a cross as well as a joy. For some priests it is a daily sharing in the agony of Christ on the Cross, for others it is a true foretaste of the eternal marriage feast in heaven. Some of the greatest priests have found that it almost impossible to proceed with the Mass, for they become totally abstracted, unaware of their surroundings or the passage of time. When St Philip Neri grew old, he used to stop altogether for an hour or so on receiving Communion, so that the servers used to blow out the candles and sneak off for breakfast before returning to help him finish. Saint Padre Pio managed to keep going, but with frequent pauses of abstraction, so that his Mass took nearly three hours. Yet people would wait outside long before dawn to attend his Mass, and never felt that the time passed slowly; 'hours were but a minute'. His Mass would be the despair of a liturgist of any age, taking so long, in total silence, with no sermon and no audience participation, but who would dare say that the most popular of all priests did not celebrate Mass properly?

The grace and power of the Mass exceeds anything the priest could possibly do through his own efforts

For the modern priest in the modern parish, the martyrdom of the Mass is far more likely to come from his parishioners: whatever he does, however he celebrates Mass, there is always someone who will complain, and do so loudly. Because the present liturgical books offer such a wide range of choices, a sensitive priest is aware that every choice he makes leaves some member of the congregation aggrieved and angry. Yet these liturgical variations are in fact peripheral to the Mass in itself: what matters is the essential sacrifice. If a priest is able to do nothing more in the day than celebrate Mass, his day is well spent, for the grace and power of the Mass exceeds anything he could possibly do through his own efforts.

Prayer and the Divine Office

Before and after and behind the Mass comes the work of prayer. The priest, like every Christian, is obliged to pray, to grow in the love of God in order to be able to grow in the love of neighbour. More than the lay Christian, the priest is obliged to pray for his people: the parish priest has a special responsibility to pray for those under his care. That is why there is an obligation for every priest and deacon to celebrate the Divine Office. This was originally the prayer of the monks, who recited the 150 Psalms every week, with readings and antiphons; it was extended to diocesan clergy in the eighth century, and became one of their major responsibilities. In the medieval communities and collegiate churches we have mentioned, some eight hours of the day was taken up with the round of prayer: that is what the founders and benefactors wanted their clergy to do, and that is why they paid them. After the Council of Trent it became less common to sing the entire Divine Office together, and increasingly priests read the various parts of the Office from the handy volume known as the Breviary. Although

> *The parish priest has a special responsibility to pray for those under his care. That is why there is an obligation for every priest and deacon to celebrate the Divine Office*

it has been drastically reduced in length, it still provides an invaluable structure for prayer during the day, which unites each individual priest or deacon with hundreds of thousands of others, clergy and laypeople, who are reciting the same psalms, reading the same passages, all over the world. When a priest is feeling tired and lonely, he can be sustained by the knowledge that in praying the Office there are so many strong voices praying along with him: when he is feeling confident and strong, his prayer can help to support some exhausted priest the other side of the world. That is why it is called the 'Prayer of the Church', even more so than the other elements in a priest's spiritual life, contemplation before the Blessed Sacrament, formal meditation, or the Rosary.

Sacraments and Sacramentals

After the Mass and prayer, the pastoral priest or deacon has the obligation to administer the sacraments to the faithful. The sacraments flow from the eucharistic identity of the priest, as representative of Christ living in His mystical Body, and therefore the most important is the administration of Holy Communion, taken to the sick and housebound as a natural extension of the Mass. This is an essentially priestly work, as the Holy Father has reminded us several times, and it is difficult to imagine what a priest could possibly be doing that is more important than bringing Christ's Body to the sick.

The presence of Christ is a healing presence: His public life was marked by healing the sick, and forgiving sinners. The priest therefore continues this ministry too, with the two healing sacraments of Penance and Anointing. The ministry to the sick in hospitals or at home is the opportunity for administering the sacrament of Anointing, whereas Penance is most often requested in church. Particularly since the 2000 Jubilee Year, people have been coming back to confession, and if a priest makes himself available at a convenient time, he will never want for souls. In many ways this is the least stressful of all priestly tasks, for there are no great arguments about how it is to be done; every person can come into the confessional and speak in their own way, and receive the individual attention of the priest. Each soul is different, and has different needs, different areas of life that require healing, encouragement or restraint, and although hearing confessions can be exhausting, and at times monotonous, there is a great consolation in being able to assure so many people of the love of God.

The sacraments of baptism and matrimony are also aspects of the life-giving presence of Christ in the Church, and are therefore appropriately celebrated by the priest who brings the Church its Eucharistic life. Nevertheless, as is well

 Sacramentals: Rites, actions and things like prayers, holy water etc. which are useful means of receiving grace but are not actual sacraments.

known, if necessary baptism can be conferred by anyone, and the sacrament of matrimony may be validly celebrated by the couple concerned without the presence or blessing of a priest if there is a serious reason. Of the sacramentals commonly performed by a priest, the funeral is the most important, since it is ideally centred on the Requiem Mass, where Christ who came to the person in Holy Communion during life welcomes him now into eternity. These occasions are times when people naturally turn to the priest, looking for the presence of Christ, and with all the difficulty and stress caused by the process of preparation, they can be real occasions of grace. In particular a funeral is a unique opportunity to preach to a church full of non-practising Catholics and non-Catholics who are actually responsive to the sermon. It is a rare moment of grace, when the Word of God can touch people who would never otherwise dream of attending a church. The ceremony of Benediction, or the longer periods of Exposition of the Blessed Sacrament now becoming so popular, are obviously an extension of the moment of adoration at the Consecration of the Mass. It is highly appropriate for the priest to be with his people during these times of adoration.

Preaching

Another vital priestly work is preaching. It is now understood that only a priest or deacon can 'preach', as opposed to a catechist or Catholic lecturer who can 'teach'. The difference is not always easy to grasp: in the past laymen were often licensed by bishops to preach, as in the case of the early Dominican friars, many of whom were not ordained. Perhaps we can define 'preaching' as delivering the discourse during Mass, which is the only opportunity there is to reach the majority of the faithful. However many evening courses we arrange, with skilled and eloquent speakers, they will only attract a tiny fraction of those who come to Sunday Mass. It is therefore a precious and privileged occasion to speak to the faithful. That is perhaps why the bulk of the seven years of priestly training is intended to equip him to proclaim the Catholic faith in the ten minutes of his weekly sermon.

A sermon needs preparation, both 'remote' and 'proximate'. Remote preparation, apart from the years endured in the seminary, means a regular inflow of ideas, from spiritual and theological reading. A priest should usually try to read for half an hour or so a day, to keep his mind alive, and to provide insights for the confessional and pastoral counselling as much as the pulpit. Proximate preparation means considering this particular occasion, the readings or the feast, and working out what to say to this particular congregation. The secret of 'great preaching' is very simple: some solid doctrinal content. People are keen to know the truth about the faith, about their own lives, about prayer.

Occasionally, during a day of recollection or retreat, it is possible to preach a longer sermon, especially if it can be detached from Mass. Although the ministry of preaching, like everything else, stems from the eucharistic presence of Christ at Mass, there is no intrinsic reason why a sermon should be actually during Mass: until the mid-twentieth-century it was in fact more common to have the sermon as part of an afternoon devotion, combined with vespers or Benediction.

Pastoral Care

Preaching and the administration of the Sacraments, as opposed to the endless preparation, do not take up very much time, leaving the priest unstructured time which can be used for anything else that occurs. Somehow a great deal of bureaucratic paperwork has been foisted on modern priests, and if they are not careful a huge proportion of the day can be taken up with routine office work, financial, building maintenance, assessment: none of these are really the priest's job at all, and all could be done far better by deacons or lay people. What is more genuinely priestly is his simple presence among the people, visiting them in their homes, in the streets, wherever they gather. Because the priest acts in the person of Christ at Mass, he reflects the presence of Christ at all times, and the mere passing along a ward, a corridor, a street, is a blessing on those around. House to house visiting may be much more difficult these days, but we should not forget how much a pastoral priest can do simply by praying for the inhabitants of each house he passes.

It is not a priest's responsibility to look after finances (*Acts* 6:2), though that burden is commonly laid upon him. The system for supporting a priest is amazingly haphazard, and confuses the Inland Revenue as much as anyone: but perhaps our present muddle makes us closer to our Master, who did not always know where to lay his head.

Special Ministries

As well as the common duties of all pastors, many priests have special areas of responsibility such as schools, hospitals, prisons or military bases. For some, these are full-time appointments, with proper salaries and fixed working hours. Full-time chaplains are usually attached to a parish (except for the military chaplains), but are not expected to be involved in the day to day grind of parish pastoral work. In most cases, however, the chaplaincy is a part-time work that has to be fitted in around the obligations of a parish. This becomes increasingly difficult with increasing regulation and bureaucracy. Each of these specialist ministries demands a particular ability,

So the Twelve called a full meeting of the disciples and addressed them, It would not be right for us to neglect the word of God so as to give out food; (Acts 6:2)

which is certainly not granted to every priest. Fundamentally, however, what all require is the same: the presence of the priest as the representative of the visible church among those who are suffering. The essential task of a chaplain is of course to celebrate Mass and distribute the sacraments to those under his care, but there is a tremendous value in simply being with people, especially those who have been estranged from the church and can take the opportunity of speaking to a chaplain in a way that they had never been able to speak to a parish priest. The presence of a priest on the wing, or on the ward, clearly visible as a priest, can be a really valuable contact for warders and nurses, domestic staff and cleaners as much as inmates or patients and their families. (That is why present trends in prison and hospital management, who want to eliminate denominational chaplaincies, are to be deplored and resisted.) In the same way a priest acting as chaplain to a school has a specifically priestly role, quite distinct from that of a teacher.

Celibacy and Women

It is impossible to write about the priesthood today without touching on the controversial question of celibacy: should it continue to be the rule in the Western Church that priests are not married? As we saw, the tradition of priests being unmarried, or separating from their wives on ordination, goes back a very long way.

The reasons given, and the advantages perceived, have varied over the centuries, ranging from the purely ritual (the Old Testament obliged priests to abstain from marriage just for a month at a time, but New Testament priests are priests for ever), to the practical (in the tenth and eleventh century there was a tendency to make priesthood hereditary, with the accompanying danger of passing on accumulated wealth to the family). In the twenty-first century we are more likely to talk about the value of the witness of a celibate priest in a world which has abandoned any attempt at self-restraint and where the wreckage of so many lives testifies to the heartbreak caused by casual promiscuity. The Catholic priest can stand as a sign of hope that there is a better way, and as a model of encouragement for those struggling to be chaste. We can also point out the practical value of detachment, for an unmarried priest, able to dedicate himself full-time to the ministry, can remain in his ministry during times of persecution and unrest, with no need to seek safety for the sake of wife and children. In developing countries, where more priests really are needed, the sheer expense of training and housing a

Celibacy: Remaining unmarried. Usually the term is used to describe someone who remains in this state for the sake of the kingdom , and in particular priests and religious. All are called to chastity; not all are called to celibacy.

married priest would put yet another obstacle in the way of ordination. There are few countries where there is not an abundance of volunteers offering themselves for the celibate priesthood; the restriction on the number who can be ordained is usually financial. But having said that, it cannot be denied that the married priests of the Eastern rites have given a heroic witness during times of persecution, and continue to serve their people with no apparent conflict of interests. It also cannot be denied that certain elements within the Church are very anxious to change the tradition, and see the ordination of married converts in England as a useful experiment. Personally I would be sad to see the ancient tradition lost, but we have to admit that the relentless campaign in the press towards abolishing celibacy does command a great deal of support. We shall see during the coming decades. But it is a decision which, once made, cannot be unmade. What is quite unacceptable is the idea that because of a perceived shortage of priests, in desperation we will ordain anything that moves, even if it is married. Marriage is not a 'second-best' - it is a holy sacrament, and not the answer to a problem.

The same applies to the even more fiercely debated question of the ordination of women. In this case we have a real problem of sacramental theology, and a clear and authoritative ruling from the Magisterium of the Church, not just a disciplinary canon. The debate will not die down, despite the divisive effects the issue has had in other denominations. What will be necessary is some serious study of theological anthropology, exploring the nature of the differentiation of the sexes in relationship to God's will for the world. Until then, the definitive answer as to why women cannot be ordained rests on the authority of the Pope, and on the clearly expressed wishes of the majority of ordinary Catholics world-wide, who feel instinctively that it would be wrong. Instinct, which Newman called the 'illative sense', can be a good guide to the will of God: the task of the theologian is to make the logical connections between what we instinctively believe and the existing agreed facts of revelation. On the other side, arguments for the ordination of women have hinged on two principles: one is the desire of particular groups for 'power', which is a very unsound base indeed: priests do not have much in the way of 'power', nor should they, they are servants of the servants of God, and someone who wants ordination as a power-base should not be ordained at all. (In the past, of course, the real power in every parish lay with Mother Superior, and everyone knew it; the disappearance of the nuns has indeed left a vacuum in our church life.) The other argument is based on the idea that Jesus and the Apostles were ignorant Hebrews who didn't know any better, and that if only he had been born in Woking in 1968 he would have instituted women priests as a matter of course. That argument is really based on the premise that Jesus is not really God, and did not possess any divine knowledge. If we do not believe that Jesus is the Son of God, there is not a lot of point in talking about priesthood, sacrament or sacrifice at all. Our religion would be nothing more than a vague ethical system, changed at the whim of each passing generation. If we do believe that Jesus is God, then part of our belief is that He was born at the right time and in the right place, that the revelation to the Jewish people was intended to become universal, and that the teaching of His apostles and their successors has always been guided by the Holy Spirit.

Scandals in the Priesthood - towards a solution

Alas, it is also impossible to write about the priesthood without touching on the problem of scandalous priests, deacons and even bishops. It is not a new problem: there was a Judas among the Apostles, and a Nicolas among the first seven Deacons, there have been Popes like Benedict IX and Julius II. Nor is it new that the enemies of the Church have seized eagerly on any evidence for moral or financial lapses to use as weapons to attack the faith. The Nazi regime was particularly skilled in working up accusations against German Catholic priests as a preparation for a whole-sale onslaught on the faith. But in recent years certain sins and accusations have become a particularly grave cause of scandal, causing great distress to faithful Catholics and glee to our enemies.

It is not a sufficient answer to point out that in fact the number of cases of grave sin among priests is actually very small in proportion to the total numbers, for even one such case is too many. What has been exposed is a serious failure on the part of some priests and bishops to take sin seriously. The old precautions which were set in place to protect the vulnerable from exploitation were cheerfully swept away in the search for spontaneity and informality; the old disciplines of prayer and penance were all too often skimped or omitted; confession was neglected in favour of amateur psychology, and the old moral laws set aside and forgotten in the rush to appear up-to-date and tolerant.

All this came at a time when the stresses and pressures on priests were greater than ever before. The tumultuous period of rapid change in the 1960s and 1970s meant that priests came under increasing pressure from disgruntled parishioners. At the same time it became common for priests to live utterly alone, for the first time in the Church's history, with neither curates nor housekeepers to help share the burden of angry callers at all hours. It is not surprising that many priests have broken down: what is surprising - dare one say miraculous - is that so many priests have actually survived, keeping their tempers, their morals and their sense of humour undamaged, and serving their people with generosity and perseverance. But when a man is put under intolerable pressure, sooner or later he will crack. The exact nature of the crack will not become apparent until too late, and may horrify him quite as much as anybody else. Some forms of breakdown are socially and morally acceptable, some are emphatically not. Surely the answer to the terrible scandals in the Church is never to allow the pressure to build up to breaking point in the first place, instead of rushing around afterwards waving cheque books and psychiatrists in the attempt to repair the damage.

That is why, as I have indicated in several places above, some reforms are urgently needed, in the selection, the training and the deployment of priests. Training should not be so narrowly academic that it omits the vital formation in the life of prayer and holiness. Priests should not be condemned to live like backstairs servants in the home of a curmudgeonly canon, until they qualify for their own parishes and thereafter must live quite alone. Nor should they be moved from place to place like pawns on a chessboard, breaking up what few supportive friendships they have been able to make, or passing on to wreak havoc in parish after parish. Increasingly people are thinking about some sort of community life as the answer to intolerable stress. With modern transport and communications, a group of priests living together can serve a wide area, comprising several present-day 'parishes', still preserving the identity of these parishes by allocating a specific priest to each. There can be various models of community to suit different characters: for some the 'sheltered housing' approach might be best, where priests have individual flats in a single complex, able to run their own households but with fellow priests across the garden, whom they can join for the occasional meal. Others would be happy in a closer community where all pray together and eat together at least a few times a week, and have a common sitting room and library, though still maintaining independent homes. Yet others are capable of living in a true religious community, where there is daily prayer together, and all eat together every day except their weekly day off. What is important for any type of community is some form of collective decision-making process, so that the juniors are not bullied, and some degree of stability so that a happy team that are functioning well together is not broken up without good reason and serious consultation. Obviously you cannot devise a system so perfect that no one needs to be good. It is impossible to think of a model of priestly life that would be absolutely ideal, but it is equally impossible to imagine one worse than what we have at present. Some sort of change is necessary.

Nor can we fall back on the glib answer which is always being trotted out that celibacy is the problem and if priests were only allowed to be married all the scandals would disappear. Marriage, as I have said already, is a holy sacrament, not a solution to a problem. If someone who has serious difficulties with his emotional life thinks he can evade them by marriage, all that will happen is that a woman and probably some children will be very badly hurt. Anyone who thinks that marriage is an easy option has obviously not been married, and has no close friends who are married. To use marriage as a means of escape would be disastrous. Nor can we say that the example of married clergy in other denominations has given us any grounds for thinking that scandals could be thereby avoided.

In all the above I have been thinking of diocesan or 'secular' priests. Religious orders, where members already live in community, are not, of course, exempt from problems, and there have been scandals even in the best of monasteries, but the problems nearly always stem from neglect of the rule, either on the part of the individual member, or of the community as a whole. That is why the history of religious orders is a continuous series of reforms, as the members return to the ideals of their founders and renew their loyalty to the vows they have professed. Most religious orders already contain the machinery for their own reform.

Prayer and Recreation

To survive as a priest - indeed to survive as a human being - a healthy balance of work, prayer and recreation is essential. It is a lie that work is prayer: time given exclusively to prayer is necessary if we are to be able to work at all. That is why the daily routine of prayer, and the personal use of the sacraments, is vital in a priest's life.

It is also vital to have some form of relaxation or recreation. In religious orders 'recreation' means a time of informal conversation together: for a diocesan priest on his own it may mean meeting other priests of a Sunday evening for a glass of something and a game of cards, or it may mean the Monday afternoon golf match. For everyone it is useful to

> *A priest's life must be grounded in prayer, or it is rootless and fruitless*

have an outside interest that can provide a counter-attraction to the pressures of pastoral life. It is normally recommended that every priest should have a regular weekly day off, and be scrupulous about not letting it become cluttered up with appointments. The priest who allows his feeling of self-importance to stop him taking time off soon ceases to be any use: God has no need of men, and the Church will continue to exist even if the priest is out every Monday.

But the Church will not continue to exist without prayer. A priest's life must be grounded in prayer, or it is rootless and fruitless. That means, apart from the obligation to celebrate the Divine Office, a priest must have time to spend alone with God. There is no better time than the morning, before the hustle of the day begins, and no better place than the church, where doorbells and telephones cannot interrupt. (No, the mobile phone is *never* taken into church.) A basis of quiet mental prayer, the recitation of the Office, and attentive reading of Scripture, means that it becomes possible to sanctify the rest of the day with frequent aspirations, short phrases of prayer often repeated, catching God's eye during work or recreation, while dealing with difficult people or in moments of happiness. If a priest is faithful in prayer, and if he uses the Sacrament of Confession regularly, then his ministry can be fruitful and his life holy. There may be few ordinary pastoral priests who have been raised to the altars of the Church, but there are still many whose lives are outstanding in holiness, and whose quiet unassuming service of God and His people continue to build up the Body of Christ in the world.

5. Further Reading

There is such an enormous range of books on the priesthood, in all its aspects, that it is difficult to know where to start. A good basic introduction to the theology of Orders is Aidan Nichols, *Holy Order,* Oscott, Birmingham, 1990. Particular problems of today are discussed in M. Hauke, *Women in the Priesthood?,* Ignatius, San Francisco, 1988, and S. Heid, *Celibacy in the Early Church,* Ignatius, San Francisco, 2000. Then on the life and spirituality of the priest there are books without end: three, almost chosen at random, are: J. C. Heenan (later Cardinal), *The People's Priest,* Sheed & Ward, London, 1951; M. Hollings, *Living Priesthood,* Mayhew-McCrimmon, Great Wakering, 1977, and R. Knox, *A Retreat for Priests,* Sheed & Ward, London 1946.

On the Sacraments:

Baptism (CTS Publications, 2004; Do 712).
Confirmation (CTS Publications, 2004; Do 713).
Eucharist (CTS Publications, 2004; Do 714).
Reconciliation (CTS Publications, 2004; Do 716).
Anointing (CTS Publications, 2004; Do 711).
Marriage (CTS Publications, 2004; Do 710).
Holy Orders (CTS Publications, 2004; Do 715).

Informative Catholic Reading

We hope that you have enjoyed reading this booklet.

If you would like to find out more about CTS booklets - we'll send you our free information pack and catalogue.

Please send us your details:

Name ....

Address ....

....

....

Postcode ....

Telephone...

Email ....

Send to: CTS, 40-46 Harleyford Road,
            Vauxhall, London
            SE11 5AY

Tel: 020 7640 0042
Fax: 020 7640 0046
Email: info@cts-online.org.uk

 **CTS**